# GREAT 20TH CENTURY EXPEDITIONS

# THOR HEYERDAHL AND
# THE KON-TIKI VOYAGE

## Philip Steele

 Dillon Press
New York

First American publication 1993 by Dillon Press, Macmillan Publishing Company, 866 Third Avenue, New York, NY 10022

Macmillan Publishing Company is part of the Maxwell Communication Group of Companies.

First published in Great Britain by Zoë Books Limited

## A ZOË BOOK

Devised and produced by
Zoë Books Limited
15 Worthy Lane
Winchester
Hampshire SO23 7AB
England

Printed in Italy by Grafedit SpA
Design: Jan Sterling, Sterling Associates
Picture research: Faith Perkins
Illustrations and maps: Gecko Limited
Production: Grahame Griffiths

10 9 8 7 6 5 4 3 2 1

Library of Congress Catalog Card Number: 93-9335

**Photographic acknowledgments**

The publishers wish to acknowledge, with thanks, the following photographic sources:

J.Allan Cash: 4, 7b; ARDEA: 19t (Ron & Valerie Taylor); Biofotos: 11b (Heather Angel), 21b (Heather Angel), 22 (J.Hoogesteger); Robert Harding Picture Library: 23b (Paul van Riel); The Kon-Tiki Museum, Oslo: 5, 6, 7t, 9t, 10r, 11t, 12, 13t, 14, 16t, 16b, 18, 19b, 21t, 23t, 24t, 24b, 25t, 25b, 26t, 29b; NHPA: 9b (Haroldo Palo), 20 (© A.N.T.); Picturepoint: title, 29t; Popperfoto: 26b, 27; South American Pictures: 8 (Kimball Morrison), 13b (Tony Morrison), 17 (Tony Morrison), 28 (Tony Morrison)

Cover photographs courtesy of The Kon-Tiki Museum, Oslo

The publishers have made every effort to trace the copyright holders, but if they have inadvertently overlooked any, they will be pleased to make the necessary arrangement at the first opportunity.

# Contents

# Riding the storms

On July 2, 1947, far out in the Pacific Ocean, six men on a **raft** were in trouble. The raft, the *Kon-Tiki*, was knocked sideways by strong waves. Three great walls of foam crashed over the raft, and water broke in through the cabin wall. Thor Heyerdahl and his crew were still about 1,125 miles (1,800 kilometers) from the nearest **Polynesian** islands and worse was to come....

▼ Strong winds and a raging sea

## Black clouds

On July 4 the **trade wind** dropped. Great black clouds billowed in the sky. Suddenly the wind **veered** around and howling gusts whipped up the crests of the waves. The raft's sail was quickly taken down and all loose items were made secure. The crew stretched canvas around the part of the cabin that housed the radio equipment.

The seas were now 16 to 26 feet (5 to 8 meters) high, running level with the top

of the mast. Rain tore into the gray and white ocean. But the *Kon-Tiki* held its own, riding the waves.

## Man overboard!

On July 21 the *Kon-Tiki* was struck by storms again. One of the crew, Herman Watzinger, was measuring the wind speed with his **anemometer**. A gale was on the way. As he tried to catch hold of a sleeping bag that was blowing away, he toppled overboard himself.

Herman tried to grab the end of the steering oar, but failed. Someone threw a lifebelt into the water. But Herman was now being swept away by high seas.

Another crew member, Knut Haugland, sprang into action. He hauled in the lifebelt with its long rope, and jumped in. He swam after Herman and finally caught up with him. The two were hauled in. Everyone was relieved, but felt grim. Two lives had so nearly been lost.

Then the storm broke in all its fury. For five days the ocean raged.

▲ Thor Heyerdahl and his crew took on the fury of the open ocean and survived.

## Counting the cost

At last the sun came out again and the sea became quieter. It was time to survey the damage. During the storms, perhaps 10,000 tons of seawater a day had washed in over the raft's **stern**. It was hardly surprising that the hemp ropes that held the raft together were beginning to wear through.

However the **balsa** logs, now slippery with seaweed, were still intact. It seemed that the sap in the trunks had stopped them from soaking up too much water. The **centerboards** were badly damaged and the steering oar was splintered. This was soon repaired with lengths of mangrove.

The *Kon-Tiki* headed westward into the sunset, following Thor Heyerdahl's dream. What was that dream, and how had it brought these six men to risk their lives on a raft in the ocean?

# A Viking for today

The Vikings lived in Scandinavia 1,000 years ago. They were seafarers who crossed and recrossed the oceans. They sailed around the coasts of Europe and westward to Greenland and North America. A modern Scandinavian was to share their love of seafaring and adventure. Thor Heyerdahl was born in Larvik, Norway, on October 6, 1914.

## Distant lands

As a child, Thor had one ambition—to be an explorer. As a student in Oslo, he chose geography and **zoology** as his subjects. Later, he studied how different peoples live, which is called **anthropology**. From

▼ Thor Heyerdahl on the island of Fatu-Hiva

1937-1938 he traveled to the distant Marquesas Islands in the Pacific Ocean, where he studied the way of life, or **culture**, of the Polynesian people. In 1939-1940 Thor moved to British Columbia, in Canada, to study the **Native American** cultures of the Pacific coast.

World War II ended Thor Heyerdahl's research. In 1940 Norway was invaded by German troops. Thor now had to lead the life of a soldier. His beloved Pacific was also torn apart by war, as the United States fought with Japan.

## Ancient peoples

Not until peacetime, after 1945, could Thor Heyerdahl return to his studies. He began to realize that peoples in different parts of the world had many things in common. They shared **myths** and **legends**. They made things in similar ways.

During his stay in the Marquesas Islands, Thor had become fascinated by strange stone carvings. They were made by the ancient peoples of Polynesia, but they reminded him of statues made far to the east, in South America. Could they be connected in some way? Perhaps, long ago, the islands of the South Pacific had been settled by people from South America?

## The story of Kon-Tiki

Thor Heyerdahl had met a very old man on Fatu-Hiva, one of the Marquesas Islands. This man's name was Tei Tetua. He told a story about Tiki, a great chief and god, whose father was the sun.

Long ago, Tiki had led Tei Tetua's ancestors to the islands from a distant land.

Thor Heyerdahl wondered if he could find any South American myths about Tiki. He read about the Incas of ancient Peru. They had ruled a great empire at the time of the Spanish invasion, four hundred years before. They worshiped a sun-god called Virakocha. Now this sun-worship probably dated back to a period before the Incas—and it seemed that the god's original name was Kon-Tiki!

Peruvian legends said that Kon-Tiki had sailed westward into the sunset, having been defeated in a mighty battle....

◀ Tei Tetua, who told Thor the story of Tiki, the Polynesian sun-god

▼ Stone statues on Easter Island

# A plan takes shape

The more Thor Heyerdahl studied, the more connections he seemed to find between the cultures of the Americas and those of the South Pacific. He was sure that the worshipers of Kon-Tiki had traveled to the Polynesian islands long ago. Perhaps later settlers had come from the region of Canada now known as British Columbia?

## Testing the ideas

In the United States, the university professors had little time for these new ideas, or theories. They knew that the peoples of ancient Peru could not build ships. They had sailed along the coasts in rafts, but these could hardly have ventured out onto the open ocean.

Or could they? Thor Heyerdahl was struck by a wild notion. If he could sail a raft from Peru to the Polynesian islands, that would surely force the experts to think again.

At this time, Thor was staying in New York City at a cheap hostel for Norwegian sailors. He questioned the seamen closely about ocean currents and **navigation**. He bought **charts** of the South Pacific. He visited a Norwegian friend who was a former sea captain. At last his mind was

▼ Was Virakocha the same god as Tiki? Thor Heyerdahl decided to find out.

▲ Members of the *Kon-Tiki* expedition: (left to right) Knut Haugland, Bengt Danielsson, Thor Heyerdahl, Erik Hesselberg, Torstein Raaby, Herman Watzinger

made up. He would build the raft himself and organize the expedition.

## Practical planning

There was no time to lose. The voyage had to be completed before the season of gales and storms swept across the southern oceans. That left only a few months in which to build the raft and find a crew.

Thor Heyerdahl's plans were welcomed by the Explorers' Club in New York. He now began to raise money and to seek support for his plan from the United States, from Norway, and other countries. He agreed to test British and American survival equipment. He promised to write articles for newspapers and to give lectures. He went to the United Nations and spoke to officials from South America.

## Six men and a parrot

For his crew, Thor Heyerdahl needed people who were tough and brave, with a sense of adventure. He also needed people who had useful skills. Above all, he needed people who would get along with each other during the long, cramped voyage.

In New York, Thor Heyerdahl met an engineer named Herman Watzinger, who was very anxious to come along. Old friends joined up too. Erik Hesselberg was a painter and guitar player. He had sailed around the world and knew all about navigation. Torstein Raaby and Knut Haugland had operated secret radio sets during the war.

Later, in South America, this all-Norwegian crew gained another member. Bengt Danielsson was a red-bearded Swedish explorer. He was very interested in Thor Heyerdahl's theories and could speak Spanish, the language spoken in Peru.

If these modern Vikings were beginning to look like a bunch of pirates, it may have been the fault of another crew member—a green parrot that also spoke Spanish!

# Trees from the rain forest

The ancient peoples of Peru made their rafts from a wood called balsa, which is tough but very light. Forests of balsa trees had once grown all along the coast, but many of these had now been destroyed.

Thor Heyerdahl and Herman Watzinger flew to the port of Guayaquil, in Ecuador. They needed whole, large

▲ The jeep, high in the Andes

balsa logs to build the raft. They were told that these still grew inland in the rain forest. Unfortunately the roads inland were flooded by the rains at this time of year. What could be done?

They decided to fly to the capital of Ecuador. The city of Quito lay high in the Andes Mountains. From there, they would be able to go down into the rain forest, although they were told that it might be a dangerous journey. There were tales of hunters who shrunk the heads of their victims, and reports of attacks by bandits.

An army captain agreed to take Thor and Herman in his jeep. They drove over high mountain passes, seeing dry desert landscapes and snowy peaks. The people of Ecuador walked by, wearing colorful ponchos and broad-brimmed hats. Donkeys and llamas trotted along the rough track.

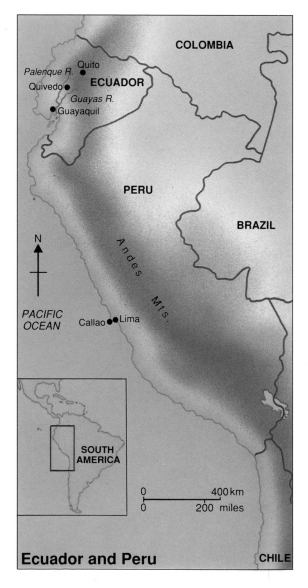

**Ecuador and Peru**

▲ Women in the Andes Mountains, spinning wool as they walk along

## Down to the rain forest

At last the jeep descended into the rain-soaked forests. This was a land of muddy rivers, of mosses and creepers. It was inhabited by deadly snakes, by stinging ants and scorpions, and by brightly colored parrots.

Thor and Herman stayed with a landowner named Don Federico von Buchwald, who lived near Quivedo on the Palenque River. Here, twelve great balsa trunks were soon felled with axes. Each was given a name from Polynesian myths and legends, and was then dragged to the river's edge by tractor.

## Floating down the river

Although balsa is a light wood, it is heavy with sap when freshly cut. The logs were rolled into the water with a great splash and were then bound together with creepers. Two crude rafts were made. Thor, Herman, and two oarsmen now steered the precious logs down the Palenque to the Guayas River.

From there, the Norwegian explorers took a paddle steamer to Guayaquil. The oarsmen made sure that the logs continued safely downstream to the port. There, Herman had them loaded on board a boat and taken south to Callao, the port for the city of Lima in Peru.

## Preparations and paperwork

In the meantime, Thor Heyerdahl flew on to Lima. There were all sorts of arrangements to be made. He went to see the president of Peru and was given permission to build the raft in the naval dockyards at Callao.

Thor then returned briefly to Washington, D.C., to sort out the growing piles of paperwork. The expedition secretary, a Norwegian woman named Gerd Vold, was kept busier and busier. After additional flights south, the whole team, including Gerd, was finally in place —in Callao beside the great Pacific Ocean.

▼ Balsa trees were cut down to build the raft.

# Building a raft

Nothing had been seen like this in Callao for hundreds of years! Dwarfed by the hulls of submarines and ships in the naval dockyards, a balsa raft was taking shape. Herman Watzinger, recovering from a neck injury, supervised the building work. Bengt Danielsson acted as interpreter.

## Timbers and ropes

The raft was an exact copy of the old Peruvian design. In the middle was the largest of the logs from the rain forest, 45 feet (14 meters) long. On either side were four smaller logs. The outer logs were the shortest, at 29 feet (9 meters). The stern of the raft was straight ended, except for a block, the **helm**, which stuck out and supported a long steering oar.

No nails or wires were used. The logs were grooved and bound together with ropes made of hemp and crossed over with nine smaller lengths of balsa. They were partly decked over with bamboo. Gaps were filled with planks of pine. These stuck down into the water and acted as a series of crude centerboards.

## Above deck

The cabin was a flimsy bamboo shack, roofed with banana leaves. The twin mast was made from tough mangrove poles and carried a canvas sail. This was soon decorated with the bearded head of the ancient sun-god, Kon-Tiki, painted in red by Erik Hesselberg. The foreman of the workers in the dockyard thought it looked more like Bengt Danielsson!

▼ Balsa logs are roped together in the water at Callao.

▲ The face of the god Kon-Tiki painted by Erik Hesselberg

## Hopes and fears

Naval officers and experts visited the docks. They shook their heads gravely and claimed that the raft would never survive in the open waters of the Pacific. They said that it would be swamped by giant waves, or that the logs would become **waterlogged** and would sink.

Thor and the crew may have had their private worries, but they carried on with their work. If rafts were good enough for the ancient Peruvians, then they were good enough for them!

## Food and stores

The crew members began to stock the raft. Boxes of army rations, together with water cans and boxes of scientific equipment, were stowed below deck between the cross beams. Baskets of fruit and coconuts were tied on deck. The radio was set up in the shack.

## The raft is named

On April 27, 1947 the raft lay ready in the calm waters of the naval dockyard. The Norwegian flag was raised on the mast, alongside the flags of the other nations who had supported the expedition. Large crowds gathered on the quayside and journalists and film crews jostled to see the strange craft.

There was only one possible name—*Kon-Tiki*. The raft was named by Gerd Vold, who smashed a coconut across its logs, to loud applause. The sail was **unfurled**.

## Farewell to Peru

The crew now went ashore for their last view of Peru. They were invited to say farewell to the president, and then they drove high into the mountains, passing old Inca ruins on the way. This was their last glimpse of land for a long time.

▼ Balsa rafts have been used on the coast of Peru since the days of the Incas.

# Setting sail

▲ At last, the *Kon-Tiki* is ready to leave the harbor at Callao.

The next day dawned, April 28, 1947. Crowds hurried down to Callao harbor to see the European explorers set out. Some people said they were crazy, others that they were brave.

The tiny *Kon-Tiki* was surrounded by yachts and small boats. Thor Heyerdahl went on board, while the rest of the crew went into town.

## Pandemonium!

A Peruvian navy tug called the *Guardian Rios* was due to tow the raft out to sea, away from the busy coastal waters. It arrived earlier than expected, and dropped anchor in the outer harbor. Its captain sent over a motor launch to tow the raft out through the smaller vessels.

In vain, Thor tried to explain that the crew was still ashore. Not understanding a word, the smiling sailors took the raft in tow. At this point the parrot escaped, and it seemed that the expedition would start in chaos!

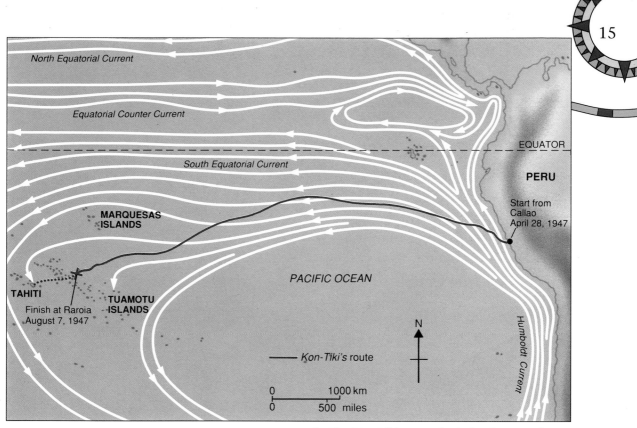

North Equatorial Current

Equatorial Counter Current

EQUATOR

South Equatorial Current

MARQUESAS ISLANDS

PERU

Start from Callao April 28, 1947

TAHITI

Finish at Raroia August 7, 1947

TUAMOTU ISLANDS

PACIFIC OCEAN

Humboldt Current

N

Kon-Tiki's route

0        1000 km
0        500  miles

▲ The *Kon-Tiki* was to be helped across the Pacific by strong ocean currents.

When Thor reached the tug he climbed aboard and explained to the captain that they were not yet ready to leave. The launch was sent off to find the other crew members. They were eventually found on the quayside, staring in disbelief at an empty mooring.

## Out to sea

By late afternoon, the *Kon-Tiki* was ready to leave. The *Guardian Rios* strained at the tow rope, and the raft bobbed past the walls of the outer harbor.

There was nearly a disaster when the tow rope snapped. The stern of the tug almost crushed the raft as it drifted out of control. Soon, however, the rope was made secure and towing could continue.

The night closed in, and ships' lights passed by in the darkness. When dawn broke, a bank of mist lay over the coast of Peru. Ahead, the sky was clear blue above the ocean swell.

## Casting off

It was time to leave the navy vessel. Thor, Erik, and Bengt took the small rubber dinghy from the *Kon-Tiki* and went on board the tugboat. There they said good-bye to the crew and checked their position on the charts. They were lying about 55 miles (90 kilometers) northwest of Callao, in the strong, cold waters of the Humboldt Current.

They knew that the Incas sailed their rafts out into these waters on fishing expeditions. But did these ancient peoples travel farther westward into the unknown ocean? It was time to find out.

The three explorers returned to the raft. With the other members of the expedition, they watched the *Guardian Rios* disappear over the horizon. Ahead lay a vast expanse of empty ocean.

# Battling with the current

At first the wind did not blow hard enough. There was a light breeze, but the sail of the *Kon-Tiki* remained slack. Herman Watzinger checked their speed. He tossed scraps of paper or chips of wood overboard and counted the seconds they took to pass the length of the raft. Progress was slow.

Then the trade wind blew up from the southeast and caught the sail. The raft heaved forward through the waves.

## Darkness and foam

Large ocean rollers now bore down on the raft and surged over the deck. It took two men to control the long steering oar, and they had to be roped for safety. That night the oarsmen saw ships' lights, but nobody out there in the darkness noticed the *Kon-Tiki*'s little lantern tossing to and fro. Each crew member had two hours at the helm,

▼ Thor Heyerdahl steering the *Kon-Tiki*

▲ Herman Watzinger checking the wind speed

followed by three hours of restless sleep.

For three days the Humboldt Current swept them along with its violent seas. The crew were exhausted. They were soaked, seasick, crusted with salt, and stiff. At last the waves quieted down. The sail was furled and there was time for everybody to sleep.

## Calling Lima

Radio contact was now made with Lima. Knut and Torstein climbed the mast with their aerials and tried tying them to balloons and kites.

The operator in Lima reported that a spotter plane was coming out from the mainland to check on their progress. Soon the crew members were in contact with Gerd Vold, who was on the aircraft. However, they could not see or hear the plane, and Gerd could not see the little raft among the great ocean waves.

## A course westward

The crew soon learned to handle the steering oar more easily and to sail the raft before the wind. They were farther north than they had planned, and were afraid of reaching the dangerous waters near the Galapágos Islands. They hoped that the rushing green seas of the Humboldt Current would carry them westward before they got that far. And so they did, carrying the *Kon-Tiki* far into the blue Pacific.

It was to be some time before the crew realized that the best way to stay on course was to use the centerboards. By raising or lowering these wooden planks they were able to steer with great accuracy.

▲ The sun sets over the Pacific Ocean.

## Riding the swell

Thor Heyerdahl and his crew became worried when the balsa logs began to soak up the seawater. Small pieces of balsa soon became waterlogged and sank. However, the great logs continued to stay afloat, and the raft seemed to ride out the ocean swell with the greatest of ease.

The hemp ropes, too, held out well. Despite all the stresses and strains they had not yet frayed or rotted. In fact, as the wet ropes cut into the soft balsa, they were protected by the wood around them. The spirits of the crew lifted and the weather was fair.

# Life on board

If you look at the earth from space, the Pacific Ocean seems to take up the whole globe. It is the world's largest ocean, covering 70,000,000 square miles (166,000,000 square kilometers). In his exciting book, *The Kon-Tiki Expedition*, Thor Heyerdahl describes the strange feeling of being afloat in this watery wilderness.

The average ocean depth is 13,611 feet (4,188 meters) and in places the sea bed plunges into deep underwater trenches. Only nine logs of balsa separated the crew of the *Kon-Tiki* from the vast, mysterious world beneath them.

Sometimes crew members rowed the rubber dinghy out from the *Kon-Tiki*. Even from a short distance away the raft looked hopelessly small. It made such a ridiculous sight that they all had to laugh. Thor Heyerdahl wrote that the raft looked more like a floating hayloft than a seagoing vessel!

## All in a day's work

After 45 days of sailing, the *Kon-Tiki* was halfway across the Pacific. **Bearings** were taken each day. A **sextant** was used to measure the angle between the sun and the horizon. A compass gave the crew directions, but, like the ancient seafarers, they also steered by the stars.

The raft needed to be checked for wear and tear. This involved swimming underneath the deck. After sailing through shark-infested waters the crew decided to make a large diving basket to protect the swimmers.

▲ The cabin provided shade and shelter.

The crew also carried out tests with the equipment they had brought with them, and made scientific experiments. The weather conditions were recorded each day, and broadcast with other radio messages to the outside world.

## Contact with the world

Amateur radio operators in the United States, and even in distant Europe, managed to pick up the **Morse code** signals of the tiny *Kon-Tiki*'s **transceiver**.

Before the voyage, Thor Heyerdahl had wondered whether to take radio equipment with them. Perhaps it was out of keeping with the spirit of those ancient seafarers? On the other hand, having a radio would make no difference to the testing of his ideas, and might well save their lives. As it happened, everyone was fascinated by the work of Torstein and Knut.

A baby flying fish at night

The parrot seemed especially thrilled, and ate a length of aerial wire! They cursed the bird, but they were all sad when the poor creature was later washed overboard by a giant wave.

## What's for dinner?

The crew cooked on deck, over a **Primus stove** in a box. All kinds of fish were

▼ Cooking a meal on board

caught every day. Tropical fruits from Peru were eaten, until they went bad. There were supplies of coconuts and sweet potatoes and oatmeal.

They used a net with a fine **mesh** to collect the tiny creatures and plants that drift in the sea in their millions. This **plankton** provided a fishy soup. Some crew members found it very tasty, but others complained that it was disgusting!

## In the cabin

Not all the time was spent at the helm or working. It was important to keep up spirits. The men took photographs, wrote in their diaries, read books, made models, or played the guitar. Sometimes they stared out at the stars and dreamed of the old gods and heroes of Polynesia. They would discuss ideas about ancient peoples long into the night, until they crawled into their sleeping bags and fell asleep.

# Creatures of the deep

▲ The whale shark. It measures up to 58 feet (18 meters) in length, and its skin can be as much as 0.5 inch (102 mm) thick.

The *Kon-Tiki* may have been far from land, but it was visited by all kinds of wildlife. Little crabs made their home in the raft's timbers. Large turtles paddled by. At night, strange shapes loomed beside the raft. These may have been huge, flapping rays or the trailing tentacles of giant squid.

## Into the air

Great whales nosed up to the raft and sleek porpoises and dolphins leaped in and out of the spray. They chased small squid, which fled at such speed that they actually flew through the air and landed on the deck! The crew used the dark, inky fluid given out by these squid to write up part of the **log book**.

Small flying fish also landed on the deck as they skimmed over the crests of the waves with their sail-like fins. Sometimes they collided with crew members, slapping them in the face.

## Fishy tales

One night encounter was with a toothy, snake-like fish with a violet-colored skin. It was a snake mackerel, a fish that lives in the depths of the ocean. It seems that it rises by night to hunt at the surface of the sea.

The crew of the *Kon-Tiki* came to know all kinds of fish, from the zebra-striped pilot fish to the sucker-mouthed remora, which attached themselves to the logs of

▲ Landing a shark on the raft

the raft. They passed ocean racers such as the tuna, the bonito, and the large swordfish with its long, pointed snout.

Some fish were caught on lines and some with **harpoons**. The crew tried eating many different kinds of fish. Rare ones were kept for scientific study. The diving basket allowed crew members to observe beautiful tropical fish as they swam beneath the raft.

## Sharks' teeth!

Sharks followed the raft, their dark fins cutting through the waves. At first the crew were very wary of them, but they soon learned how to catch them. They even treated some like pets, tossing them scraps of food. Even so, it was important that they never forgot about those razor-sharp teeth. As soon as fish guts were thrown overboard the water would boil with threshing, silver-blue bodies and snapping jaws.

## A sea giant

On May 24, Knut Haugland was washing his clothes in the sea when he yelled at the top of his voice. He was staring into the spotted face of the world's biggest fish. The rare whale shark is a gentle giant, which feeds only on plankton and other small creatures. Its huge bulk can easily overturn a fishing boat—or a raft.

The shark circled the *Kon-Tiki* for about an hour, but to the crew it seemed longer. In the end, Erik Hesselberg flung a harpoon at the giant. It dove and swam away.

## Stars of the sea

At night the inky black waves sparkled as they rolled by the raft. This was not reflected light from the moon and stars. Many **algae**, and small sea creatures such as shrimp which live in the plankton, glow in the dark. This light is known as **phosphorescence**. Beneath the waves larger blobs of light could be seen, for many fish can produce their own light.

▼ Turtles swim over to the balsa raft.

# Land ahoy!

▲ Frigate birds mean that land is not far away.

Storms threatened the lives of the crew throughout the month of July. They also made it very uncertain where the *Kon-Tiki* would finally reach land. As July passed, there were more and more sightings of frigate birds and boobies, which suggested that land was not too far away. The raft seemed to be approaching Fatu-Hiva, the island where Thor Heyerdahl had first heard the legend of Tiki, ten years before.

However, a wind from the northeast drove the raft southward toward the Tuamotu Islands. The wind dropped.

Clouds could be seen on the horizon, the sort of clouds that form only over land.

## Puka-Puka!

At dawn on July 30, 1947 Herman Watzinger climbed up the rope ladder to the mast. Ten minutes later he gave a shout. A smudge of land lay on the horizon! As the sun rose, they approached the island of Puka-Puka.

The raft was spotted by the islanders, who lit a fire to signal a welcome.

▲ The fork of the mast was a good lookout spot.

Unfortunately, as a thick column of smoke arose, it became clear that strong currents would prevent the raft from being steered over to the island.

## On to Angatau

The next morning, two new islands came into view. They were Fangahina and Angatau. The crew steered for Angatau, only too aware of the dangerous currents and **coral reefs**. Soon they saw beautiful beaches and coconut palms. All day they tried to approach the island through the reef, but without success.

That evening Angatau islanders paddled out to them in canoes. These were the first humans the crew had met in 97 days. The Polynesians could not believe that the Europeans had no outboard motor! They willingly agreed to tow the raft in with their canoes. Knut Haugland went to help them in the rubber dinghy.

As darkness fell, a fire was lit on the reef to mark the route inshore. The islanders strained at their paddles and sang, but they could not move the raft against the strong currents. They had to give up, and the *Kon-Tiki* started to drift away from the reef.

## Knut returns

As the Angatau islanders waved good-bye, Thor Heyerdahl worried about Knut, who was still near the coral reef. It was not safe for him to row out on his own in the rubber dinghy. Desperately, the crew signaled to him with a lamp, in Morse code.

It was half past ten before they heard the sound of voices in the night. Three canoes appeared out of the darkness, with the dinghy in tow. Knut rejoined the *Kon-Tiki* and said good-bye to the islanders.

## Back to sea

For three more days the *Kon-Tiki* drifted. The crew saw no more islands and tried to steer northward of the dangerous reefs that they knew lay ahead. The wind changed and it began to rain.

What would they do if they were shipwrecked? They prepared the raft and made plans for their survival.

▼ The crew did not know where the *Kon-Tiki* would land.

# Shipwreck

It was the morning of August 7, 1947 and 101 days had passed since the *Kon-Tiki* had left Peru. The tiny raft had covered 4,625 miles (7,400 kilometers) of ocean. Now at last it was heading straight for a group of islands.

There was just one problem. Between the raft and the islands lay the Raroia coral reef, a barrier of razor-sharp rock and roaring surf. The crew had no choice but to prepare for a crash landing. Torstein Raaby tapped the key on the radio transceiver in order to tell the world where they were landing.

## Impact!

The centerboards were lifted and the sail was taken down. The anchor was trailed on its rope to act as a brake. Anything of value was tied up in waterproof bags.

The surf boomed ahead of them. As a giant wave lifted them high into the air, they cut the anchor and swept forward. The crew clung desperately to the raft as

▼ The *Kon-Tiki* was wrecked on a reef.

▲ The deck was strewn with wreckage.

they hit a great wall of green water. It surged over them, cracking the wood like matchsticks. The raft ground into the reef. Blinding salt water spilled and sprayed. Thor Heyerdahl later described it as a "witches' kitchen."

Where was everyone? At first Thor could only see Herman's body, lying flat on the cabin roof. The mast was smashed, the steering oar was in splinters, and the deck was ripped up. But the nine balsa logs were still in one piece and had withstood the impact.

Gradually, people crawled out of the water, sore but happy. All the crew members were safe and they had landed at last in Polynesia!

## Paradise lagoon

Beyond the reef lay a perfect **lagoon**. Its blue waters were filled with beautiful fish. Beyond that lay a couple of islands, one of which seemed to offer an ideal base for the crew.

The rubber dinghy was found on the reef and it was used to **salvage** goods that had survived the wreck. The crew took the

▲ Thor Heyerdahl being greeted by Chief Teka on Raroia

radio and the stove. Then they lay on the warm sand and drank fresh coconut milk.

No one lived on the island, but the six men soon made themselves at home. They swam and explored the lagoon. They dried out the radio parts and at last managed to get in touch with the outside world.

## The end of the adventure

Days passed, and then canoes from a nearby island arrived. The islanders had seen the crew's fire from a village on the far side of the lagoon, and wreckage from the raft had been washed ashore. The Raroians gave the crew a friendly welcome.

Bengt went off with them and returned the next day with the chief of all the islands, named Teka. The following days were passed in dancing and feasting. Everybody wanted to hear about the white men who knew of the god Tiki and who had sailed across the ocean on a *pae-pae*, or raft.

What of the *Kon-Tiki* itself? It was lifted off the reef by a high tide, and brought safely into the lagoon. When at last a **schooner** took Thor Heyerdahl and his crew off to Tahiti, the battered old *Kon-Tiki* was in tow.

▼ The crew plant a coconut from Peru in Polynesia.

# Further expeditions

▲ Thor Heyerdahl and his team with an Easter Island statue during the Aku-Aku expedition, 1955-1956

Thor Heyerdahl and his crew left Tahiti and returned to the United States on a Norwegian steamer. The *Kon-Tiki* came too —on the deck.

Thor Heyerdahl wrote about the great adventure in his book, *The Kon-Tiki Expedition*. It was published in Norwegian in 1948 and in English in 1950. It became a best-seller around the world, and in 1951 a film was made about the voyage. In 1949 a *Kon-Tiki* museum was set up in Oslo, where people could see the repaired balsa raft for themselves.

## Back to the Pacific

The *Kon-Tiki* expedition was not the end of the story. Thor Heyerdahl continued to wonder about the peoples of the ancient world, and how cultures might have been transferred from one continent to another.

He returned to South America and visited the Galápagos Islands. He spent 1955-1956 on Easter Island. There he examined the huge carved stone heads that had guarded the island for hundreds of years. Who had put them there, and why? Thor Heyerdahl wrote about these mysteries in a book called *Aku-Aku*, which was published in 1958.

## Across the Atlantic Ocean

During the 1960s Thor Heyerdahl turned his attention to possible links between Africa and the Americas. He studied ancient stone statues and pyramids in Egypt and in Central and South America.

▼ *Ra II* being pulled to the road in Egypt

He also learned how boats were built from bundles of reeds in both parts of the world.

In 1969-1970 he built large boats from a type of reed called papyrus, that grows on the Nile River. He followed an ancient Egyptian design. The first boat, *Ra*, sank at sea. But the second, *Ra II*, was successfully sailed all the way from Morocco, in North Africa, to the Caribbean island of Barbados. Could the ancient Egyptians have crossed the Atlantic thousands of years ago?

## Asia and Africa

The years of 1977-1978 saw Thor Heyerdahl in the Middle East. In the marshland of southern Iraq reeds were traditionally used to build both boats and

▲ Thor Heyerdahl in front of *Ra II*

houses. Soon another expedition was under way, as Thor Heyerdahl's reed-built *Tigris* sailed south from Qurnah, bound for distant Djibouti on the coast of Africa.

These were the waters described long ago in the *Arabian Nights*. Like Sinbad the Sailor, the hero of one of those fantastic tales, Thor Heyerdahl had now seen many strange sights in distant parts of the world.

## Mysteries in stone

During the 1980s Thor Heyerdahl visited the Maldive Islands, the long chain of islands in the Indian Ocean.

He also returned to Easter Island. There, the great stone faces still stared out to sea, keeping their ancient secrets to themselves....

# Ancient mysteries

After the *Kon-Tiki* and Easter Island expeditions, Thor Heyerdahl was convinced that the Polynesian islands had been settled long ago by pale-skinned strangers from South America. He believed that they had clashed with later settlers from British Columbia.

However, all the *Kon-Tiki* voyage had really proved was that it was possible to sail a raft from Peru to the Polynesian islands. He had not proved that the ancient Peruvians had actually done so.

▼ Boats built from reed are still used in Peru.

## Who were the early Polynesians?

Today, most experts think that the Polynesian islands were in fact settled from the west, not from the Americas. Scientists have studied the physical makeup of the Polynesian people and considered how much they resemble other peoples of the Pacific and the Americas. They have also compared their languages with others.

It seems fairly certain that the Polynesians are related to a people who lived in the region of the Philippines and

▲ The raft is displayed at Oslo's *Kon-Tiki* Museum.

eastern Indonesia about 5,000 years ago. These people moved into the western Pacific and had contact with the Melanesian peoples who lived there.

From about 1600 B.C. onward the early Polynesians probably began to sail eastward. By A.D. 1000 they had settled the Pacific from New Zealand to Hawaii to Easter Island, an area of nearly 8 million square miles (20 million square kilometers). This was one of the most remarkable movements of people in history.

## Thor and his theories

Thor Heyerdahl may have been mistaken in his beliefs about the movement of ancient peoples through the Pacific, but much of his work remains very useful.

It does seem likely that certain islands were visited by peoples from the Americas, even if these were not the first Polynesians. Many of the similarities with South American and British Columbian cultures remain a mystery that may never be completely explained.

## Looking back

How useful was the voyage of the *Kon-Tiki*? Since we can now be fairly certain that the first Polynesians were not the raft-sailors of the Humboldt Current, was it a waste of time?

Not at all. The expedition started an exciting debate about the way in which ideas and ways of life have spread around the world. The voyages of the *Kon-Tiki* and the *Ra II* showed that even the simplest, most **primitive** craft, such as rafts and reed boats, can travel across open ocean.

Today we often forget that the people of long ago were intelligent and able. They traveled and traded over long distances, even when that required great personal bravery.

## A great adventure

Perhaps the real worth of the *Kon-Tiki* expedition should be seen in the way that Thor Heyerdahl and his crew recaptured that ancient spirit of adventure.

In 1947 they were not followed by a fleet of rescue boats like some of today's explorers. They traveled alone, with only basic equipment. They took on the great and powerful ocean, and won. The Vikings would have been proud of them.

▼ Thor Heyerdahl as an older man

# Glossary

**algae:** types of water plants that vary from tiny floating specks to large seaweeds

**anemometer:** an instrument for measuring the speed of the wind

**anthropology:** the study of human development, customs, and beliefs

**balsa:** a tree that grows in South America. Its wood becomes very light when dry. It was once used for building aircraft and is still popular with model makers.

**bearing:** in navigation, the accurate measurement, in degrees, of a position in relation to north and south

**centerboard:** a board or keel projecting from the bottom of a boat or raft. It can be raised or lowered.

**chart:** a map showing details of coastlines, currents, and the ocean floor

**coral reef:** an underwater ridge made of coral rock. This rock is formed from the chalky casings of corals, tiny animals that live in warm waters.

**culture:** in anthropology, the word "culture" means the way of life followed by a group of people, and passed down from one generation to the next

**harpoon:** a barbed spear on a line, used to catch large fish or whales

**helm:** the part of a vessel that controls the steering—an oar, a rudder, or a wheel

**lagoon:** an area of shallow, calm sea lying between a reef and the shore

**legend:** a traditional story that cannot be checked historically

**log book:** the written record of a ship's or aircraft's voyage

**mesh:** closely woven netting that catches very small sea creatures

**Morse code:** a method of sending signals using dots and dashes, or short and long flashes of a lamp

**myth:** a traditional tale about gods and goddesses or magical events

**Native Americans:** the peoples who lived in the Americas before the arrival of the European explorer Christopher Columbus in 1492. They include the Inuit and the peoples whom Columbus mistakenly called "Indians."

**navigation:** setting and following a course across the sea in a vessel, or through the sky in an aircraft

**phosphorescence:** the giving out of light by objects at low temperatures

| | |
|---|---|
| **plankton:** | tiny plants and creatures that float in the water, drifting with the ocean currents |
| **Polynesian:** | to do with the people or islands of the South Pacific. "Polynesia" means "many islands." Polynesians include the Maoris of New Zealand and the Hawaiians. Non-Polynesian inhabitants of the Pacific islands include Micronesians and Melanesians. |
| **primitive:** | not making use of modern technology |
| **Primus stove:** | a small portable stove fueled by paraffin |
| **raft:** | a floating platform used for traveling on lakes, rivers, or seas |
| **salvage:** | to recover a ship or its cargo from the sea |
| **schooner:** | a sailing ship with two or more masts |
| **sextant:** | an instrument used in navigation. It measures the height of the sun above the horizon. |
| **stern:** | the back end of a ship or raft |
| **trade winds:** | winds that blow on either side of the Equator. Before ships had engines, they helped merchant ships sail around the world at speed. The trade winds used by the *Kon-Tiki* blow from the southeast. |
| **transceiver:** | equipment for sending and receiving radio signals |
| **unfurl:** | to let out a sail or a flag so that it catches the wind |
| **veering:** | a change in the wind's direction |
| **waterlogged:** | soaked or saturated with water |
| **zoology:** | the study of animal life |

## Further Reading

Heyerdahl, Thor. *Aku-Aku*. New York: Ballantine, 1974.

— *Easter Island*. New York: Random House, 1989.

— *Fatu-Hiva: Back to Nature on a Pacific Island*. New York: Doubleday, 1975.

— *Kon-Tiki*. New York: Simon & Schuster, 1987.

— *The Ra Expeditions*. New York: Doubleday, 1971.

Heyerdahl, Thor and Christopher Ralling. *Kon-Tiki Man: An Illustrated Biography*. New York: Chronicle Books, 1991.

# Index